1 Master Mix

51 Cakes & Cupcakes

Copyright © 2003 CQ Products
Waverly, IA 50677
All rights reserved.
No part of this book may be reproduced or transmitted in any form or by any means, electronic or mechanical, including photocopying, recording or by any information storage and retrieval system, without permission in writing from the publisher.

Printed in the United States of America
by G&R Publishing Co.

Distributed By:

507 Industrial Street
Waverly, IA 50677

ISBN 1-56383-146-5
Item #3602

How to Use This Book

Begin by stirring up a batch of the Master Mix to store in your cupboard. When you find yourself craving homemade cakes or cupcakes, just start with a few cups of your Master Mix then add your wet ingredients and yummy extras. One Master Mix makes it a snap to whip up a tasty, homemade cake or scrumptious cupcakes for dessert!

All of the cupcake recipes make approximately 2 dozen cupcakes.

Recipes shown on the front cover:

* Pumpkin Spice Cupcakes with Cream Cheese Frosting.. 86,5
* Pineapple Upside Down Cake 8
* Chocolate Cupcakes with Cream Cheese Frosting, ... 82,5
  chocolate chips and toffee pieces
* Lemon Cream Cupcakes with Confectioners Glaze 72,4
  and lemon zest
* Carrot Raisin Spice Cupcakes with Confectioners........ 94,4
  Glaze and cinnamon

Master Mix for Cakes & Cupcakes

Makes enough for 6 to 8 cake or cupcake recipes.

13 1/3 C. flour
6 T. baking powder
1 1/2 T. salt
8 C. sugar
2 tsp. soda

1 tsp. vanilla
2 T. vinegar
2 C. water

2

Combine flour, baking powder and salt, mixing thoroughly with a wire whisk, making sure to break up any flour lumps. Add sugar and again mix thoroughly until evenly combined.

Store mix in a tightly covered container in a cool, dry place.

Before using, be sure to give the mix a good stir as ingredients of different particle size may settle at different levels over time.

The Master Mix for Cakes & Cupcakes will keep for three to four months.

Frosting & Glazes

Chocolate Glaze

1/3 C. chocolate chips
1 T. butter
1 1/2 T. milk
1/2 C. powdered sugar

In a double broiler, melt chocolate chips with butter*. Allow the chocolate mixture to cool slightly, then, with a wire whisk, stir in milk and powdered sugar.

*The chocolate chips and butter can also be melted in the microwave, but must be done very carefully as chocolate can easily be overheated in a microwave which makes the chocolate stiff instead of a smooth liquid.

Confectioners Glaze

1/4 C. milk
1 to 1 1/2 C. powdered sugar

In a small mixing bowl, combine milk with powdered sugar, depending on your desired consistency. Mix with a wire whisk, and drizzle over cake or cupcakes. This simple glaze can be flavored with vanilla or any extract. Juice or liqueur may also be substituted for some or all of the milk.

Cream Cheese Frosting

1-8 oz. cream cheese, cold
5 T. butter, softened
2 tsp. vanilla
2 to 2 1/2 C. powdered sugar

In a mixing bowl, beat cream cheese, butter and vanilla on high speed until smooth. Add the powdered sugar 1/3 at a time, each time beating just until smooth.

Buttery Chocolate-Chocolate Chip Cake

1 C. butter, softened
4 C. Master Mix
1/4 C. baking cocoa
2 eggs
1 egg yolk
1 tsp. vanilla
1 C. milk
1/2 C. sour cream
1 1/2 C. chocolate chips

Preheat oven to 350°. Grease and flour cake pan.

In a large mixing bowl and using two knives, a pastry blender or a wire whisk, cut butter into the Master Mix and cocoa until the mixture resembles fine crumbs.

Make a well in the center of the mixture and add eggs, egg yolk, vanilla, milk and sour cream. Mix on low speed for 1 minute. Stop to scrape the sides of the bowl. Mix again on medium speed for 2 minutes. Batter should be smooth with no visible lumps. Stir in chocolate chips.

Pour batter into a 9"x13" pan. Bake for 30 to 35 minutes or until a toothpick inserted in the center comes out clean.

Pineapple Upside Down Cake

4 1/3 C. Master Mix
2/3 C. shortening
2 eggs
1 C. milk
1 tsp. vanilla
Topping:
1/2 C. butter, melted
2/3 C. brown sugar
1-16 oz. can pineapple slices, drained
1/2 C. maraschino cherries

Preheat oven to 350°.

In a large mixing bowl and using two knives, a pastry blender or a wire whisk, cut shortening into the Master Mix until the mixture resembles fine crumbs.

Make a well in the center of the mixture and add eggs, milk and vanilla. Mix on low speed for 1 minute. Stop to scrape the sides of the bowl. Mix again on medium speed for 2 minutes. Batter should be light and smooth with no visible lumps.

For the topping, pour melted butter into a 9"x13" pan. Stir in brown sugar until well mixed. Arrange pineapple slices on top of the butter mixture. Place cherries in the center of each slice and between slices then pour batter over the top.

Bake for 30 to 35 minutes or until a toothpick inserted in the center comes out clean. Remove from oven and allow to cool for 5 minutes. Invert cake onto a serving tray, lightly tapping the bottom of the pan to make sure cake is released before removing pan.

Top with Confectioners Glaze (recipe on page 5).

Strawberry Bundt Cake

2/3 C. vegetable oil
2/3 C. milk
3 1/2 C. Master Mix
3 eggs
1 pkg. (4 serving size) strawberry jello

Preheat oven to 350°. Grease and flour Bundt pan.

In a large mixing bowl, combine oil, milk, Master Mix, eggs and jello. Mix on low speed for 1 minute. Stop to scrape the sides of the bowl. Mix again on medium speed for 1 minute. Batter should be light and smooth with no visible lumps.

Pour batter into a Bundt pan. Bake for 35 to 40 minutes or until the top springs back when lightly touched. Remove from oven and allow to cool for 5 minutes. Invert cake onto a serving tray, lightly tapping the bottom of the pan to make sure cake is released before removing pan.

Top with whipped topping and garnish with sliced strawberries (or toss chopped frozen strawberries with 1/4 cup sugar and drizzle over whipped topping).

Lemon Pound Cake

3 eggs
3/4 C. milk
1 tsp. vanilla
3 C. Master Mix
1 1/2 C. butter, softened
1 T. lemon zest

Preheat oven to 350°. Grease and flour loaf pan.

In a small mixing bowl, combine eggs, milk and vanilla. Set aside.

In a large mixing bowl and using two knives, a pastry blender or a wire whisk, cut butter into the Master Mix until the mixture resembles fine crumbs.

Make a well in the center of the mixture and add lemon zest and half of the egg mixture. Mix on high speed for exactly 1 minute. Batter should be light colored and somewhat fluffy. Mix in half of the remaining egg mixture at low speed for about 20 seconds. Mix in remaining egg mixture at low speed for another 20 seconds.

Pour batter into a loaf pan. Bake for 50 to 60 minutes or until a toothpick inserted in the center comes out clean. You may also pour batter into a Bundt pan and reduce baking time by 5 to 10 minutes or until the top springs back when lightly touched. Remove from oven and allow to cool for 5 minutes. Invert cake onto a serving tray, lightly tapping the bottom of the pan to make sure cake is released before removing pan.

Black Forest Cake

3/4 C. shortening
3/4 C. baking cocoa
3 1/4 C. Master Mix
2 eggs
1 tsp. vanilla
1 C. milk
1-15 oz. can cherry pie filling
1-8 oz. tub whipped topping

Preheat oven to 350°. Grease and flour cake pan.

In a large mixing bowl and using two knives, a pastry blender or a wire whisk, cut shortening into the Master Mix and cocoa until the mixture resembles fine crumbs.

Make a well in the center of the mixture and add eggs, vanilla and milk. Mix on low speed for 1 minute. Stop to scrape the sides of the bowl. Mix again on medium speed for 2 minutes. Batter should be smooth with no visible lumps.

Pour batter into a 9"x13" pan. Bake for 35 to 40 minutes or until a toothpick inserted in the center comes out clean. You may also pour batter into two 8" round layer cake pans and bake for 30 to 35 minutes or until a toothpick inserted in the center comes out clean.

Allow cake to cool completely. Top with cherry pie filling and then whipped topping. Refrigerate leftovers.

Sour Cream Chocolate Chip Cake

3 C. Master Mix
3/4 C. butter, softened
1 C. sour cream
2 eggs
1 tsp. vanilla
1 C. miniature chocolate chips

Preheat oven to 350°. Grease and flour cake pan.

In a large mixing bowl, combine Master Mix and butter. Mix on low speed for 1 1/2 minutes.

In a separate bowl, combine sour cream, eggs and vanilla and stir until well mixed.

Make a well into the center of the crumb mixture and add half of the egg mixture. Mix on medium speed for 1 minute. Stop to scrape the sides of the bowl. Add remaining egg mixture and mix on medium speed for another minute. Stir in chocolate chips.

Pour batter into a 9"x13" pan. Bake for 30 to 35 minutes or until a toothpick inserted in the center comes out clean.

Oatmeal Cake

1 1/2 C. boiling water
1 C. quick oats
1/2 C. margarine
3 C. Master Mix
2 eggs
1 tsp. vanilla
1 tsp. cinnamon
1/2 tsp. nutmeg

Preheat oven to 350°. Grease and flour cake pan.

Combine oats and boiling water; set aside, allowing to cool slightly.

In a large mixing bowl and using two knives, a pastry blender or a wire whisk, cut margarine into the Master Mix until the mixture resembles fine crumbs.

In a separate bowl, combine eggs, vanilla, cinnamon and nutmeg and beat lightly.

Make a well in the center of the crumb mixture and add egg mixture and oatmeal mixture. Mix on low speed for 1 minute or until just combined.

Pour batter into a 9"x13" pan. Bake for 30 to 35 minutes or until a toothpick inserted in the center comes out clean.

Apple Walnut Upside Down Cake

1/2 C. margarine, slightly softened
3 1/4 C. Master Mix
3/4 C. ground or very finely chopped walnuts

1/2 tsp. cinnamon
1/4 tsp. nutmeg
2 eggs
1 C. milk
1 tsp. vanilla

Topping:
4 or 5 medium-sized apples

1/2 C. butter
1 C. sugar

In a large mixing bowl and using two knives, a pastry blender or a wire whisk, cut margarine into the Master Mix until the mixture resembles fine crumbs. Stir in walnuts, cinnamon and nutmeg.

Make a well in the center of the mixture and add eggs, milk and vanilla. Mix on low speed for 1 minute. Stop to scrape the sides of the bowl. Mix again on medium speed for 2 minutes.

Preheat oven to 350°.

To prepare topping, peel and slice apples. In a 10" cast iron skillet (used for baking the whole cake), melt butter. Sprinkle the sugar over the butter then arrange apple slices to lean against the sides of the pan. Fill the bottom of the pan with the remaining apple slices.

Cook on high heat for 8 to 10 minutes. Syrup should begin to darken to an amber color. Remove pan from heat. Flip apples over with a fork and cook for another 5 minutes. Remove from heat and pour batter over top.

Bake for 25 to 35 minutes or until a toothpick inserted in the center comes out clean. Remove from oven and allow to cool for 5 minutes. Invert cake onto a serving tray, lightly tapping the bottom of the skillet to make sure cake is released before removing pan.

White Cake

3/4 C. shortening
3 1/2 C. Master Mix
3 egg whites, lightly beaten
1 C. milk
1 tsp. vanilla

Preheat oven to 350°. Grease and flour cake pan.

In a large mixing bowl and using two knives, a pastry blender or a wire whisk, cut shortening into the Master Mix until the mixture resembles fine crumbs.

Make a well in the center of the mixture and add egg whites, milk and vanilla. Mix on low speed for 1 minute. Stop to scrape the sides of the bowl. Mix again on medium speed for 2 minutes. Batter should be light and smooth with no visible lumps.

Pour batter into a 9"x13" pan. Bake for 30 to 35 minutes or until a toothpick inserted in the center comes out clean. You may also pour batter into two 8" round layer cake pans and bake for 25 to 30 minutes or until a toothpick inserted in the center comes out clean.

German Chocolate Cake

1/2 C. vegetable oil
3 1/2 C. Master Mix
1 pkg. (4 serving size)
    chocolate or
    chocolate fudge
    pudding mix

3 eggs
1 1/4 C. milk
1 tsp. vanilla

Topping:
1 C. evaporated milk
1 C. sugar
3 egg yolks
1/2 C. margarine
1 tsp. vanilla

1 1/3 C. flaked
    coconut
1 C. chopped
    pecans

Preheat oven to 350°. Grease and flour cake pan.

In a large mixing bowl, combine oil, Master Mix, pudding mix, eggs, milk and vanilla. Mix on medium speed for 1 minute. Stop to scrape the sides of the bowl. Mix again on low speed for 1 minute. Batter should be smooth with no visible lumps.

Pour batter into a 9"x13" pan. Bake for 30 to 35 minutes or until a toothpick inserted in the center comes out clean.

For the topping, combine evaporated milk, sugar, egg yolks, margarine and vanilla in a saucepan and cook over low heat, stirring constantly, until mixture begins to thicken. Remove from heat and allow to cool slightly.

Add mixture to coconut and pecans in a mixing bowl. Beat by hand or with mixer until topping reaches a good spreading consistency. Spread over cooled cake.

Lemon Bundt Cake

2/3 C. vegetable oil
4 C. Master Mix
3 eggs
1 C. water
1 pkg. (4 serving size) lemon jello

Glaze:
1/4 C. orange juice
2/3 C. powdered sugar

Preheat oven to 350°. Grease and flour Bundt pan.

In a large mixing bowl, combine oil, Master Mix, eggs, water and jello. Mix on low speed for 1 minute. Stop to scrape the sides of the bowl. Mix again on medium speed for 1 minute. Batter should be light and smooth with no visible lumps.

Pour batter into a Bundt pan. Bake for 35 to 40 minutes or until the top springs back when lightly touched. Remove from oven and allow to cool for 5 minutes. Invert cake onto a serving tray, lightly tapping the bottom of the pan to make sure cake is released before removing pan.

For the glaze, in a small bowl and using a wire whisk, mix orange juice with powdered sugar. The glaze should be thin, but not watery. Drizzle over the top of the cake while still warm.

Pumpkin Chiffon Cake

5 egg yolks
1/2 C. vegetable oil
1 1/4 C. canned pumpkin
1 tsp. cinnamon
1/2 tsp. ginger
1/2 tsp. nutmeg
1/4 tsp. cloves
3 1/2 C. Master Mix
5 egg whites
1/2 tsp. cream of tartar
1/4 C. sugar

Preheat oven to 325°. Grease and flour Bundt pan.

In a large mixing bowl, combine egg yolks, oil, pumpkin, cinnamon, ginger, nutmeg and cloves. Mix on high speed for 30 seconds or until smooth. Add Master Mix and mix again on high speed for 30 seconds or until smooth.

In a separate mixing bowl, combine egg whites, cream of tartar and sugar on high speed until mixture forms soft peaks, but isn't dry. With a spatula, take 1/4 of the egg white mixture and fold into batter to loosen. Fold in the remaining egg white mixture.

Pour batter into a Bundt pan. Bake for 50 to 60 minutes or until the top springs back when lightly touched. Remove from oven and allow to cool for 5 minutes. Invert cake onto a serving tray, lightly tapping the bottom of the pan to make sure cake is released before removing pan.

Chocolate Cake

3/4 C. shortening
3 C. Master Mix
3/4 C. baking cocoa
3 eggs
1 C. milk
1 tsp. vanilla
2 oz. semi-sweet baking
   chocolate, melted

Preheat oven to 350°. Grease and flour cake pan.

In a large mixing bowl and using two knives, a pastry blender or a wire whisk, cut shortening into the Master Mix and cocoa until the mixture resembles fine crumbs.

Make a well in the center of the mixture and add eggs, milk and vanilla. Mix on low speed for 1 minute. Stop to scrape the sides of the bowl. Mix again on medium speed for 2 minutes. Batter should be smooth with no visible lumps. Stir in melted chocolate.

Pour batter into a 9"x13" pan. Bake for 30 to 35 minutes or until a toothpick inserted in the center comes out clean. You may also pour batter into two 8" round layer cake pans and bake for 25 to 30 minutes or until a toothpick inserted in the center comes out clean.

Applesauce Cake

3/4 C. shortening
3 1/2 C. Master Mix
2 eggs
1/2 C. sour cream
1 tsp. cinnamon
1/2 tsp. cloves
1 1/2 C. applesauce
1 C. raisins

Preheat oven to 350°. Grease and flour cake pan.

In a large mixing bowl and using two knives, a pastry blender or wire whisk, cut shortening into the Master Mix until the mixture resembles fine crumbs.

Make a well in the center of the mixture and add eggs, sour cream, cinnamon, cloves and applesauce. Mix on low speed for 1 minute. Stop to scrape the sides of the bowl. Mix again on medium speed for 2 minutes. Stir in raisins.

Pour batter into a 9"x13" pan. Bake for 35 to 40 minutes or until a toothpick inserted in the center comes out clean.

Banana-Coconut Cake

4 C. Master Mix
3 eggs
2/3 C. milk
1/2 C. vegetable oil
1 C. mashed bananas (about
   3 bananas)
1 C. flaked coconut
1 tsp. coconut extract or
   coconut flavoring

Preheat oven to 350°. Grease and flour cake pan.

In a large mixing bowl, combine Master Mix, eggs, milk, oil, bananas, coconut and coconut extract. Mix on low speed for 1 minute. Stop to scrape the sides of the bowl. Mix again on medium speed for 1 minute.

Pour batter into a 9"x13" pan. Bake for 30 to 40 minutes or until a toothpick inserted in the center comes out clean.

Chiffon Cake

5 egg yolks
3/4 C. water
1/2 C. vegetable oil
1 tsp. vanilla
3 1/2 C. Master Mix
5 egg whites
1/2 tsp. cream of tartar
1/4 C. sugar

Preheat oven to 325°. Grease and flour Bake pan.

In a large mixing bowl, combine egg yolks, water, oil and vanilla. Mix on low speed for 1 minute or until smooth. Stop to scrape the sides of the bowl. Add Master Mix, and mix again on high speed for 20 to 30 seconds or until smooth.

In a separate bowl, combine egg whites, cream of tartar and sugar. Mix on high speed until mixture forms soft peaks, but isn't dry. With a spatula, take 1/4 of the egg white mixture and fold into batter to loosen. Fold in the remaining egg white mixture.

Pour batter into a Bundt pan. Bake for 50 to 60 minutes or until top springs back when lightly touched. Remove from oven and allow to cool for 5 minutes. Invert cake onto a serving tray, lightly tapping the bottom of the pan to make sure cake is released before removing pan.

Top with Confectioners Glaze (recipe on page 5).

Chocolate Bundt Cake

1/2 C. vegetable oil
3 3/4 C. Master Mix
1 pkg. (4 serving size) chocolate or
    chocolate fudge pudding mix
3 eggs
1 C. sour cream
1/2 C. water
1 tsp. vanilla

Preheat oven to 350°. Grease and flour Bundt pan.

In a large mixing bowl, combine oil, Master Mix, pudding mix, eggs, sour cream, water and vanilla. Mix on medium speed for 1 minute. Stop to scrape the sides of the bowl. Mix again on low speed for 1 minute. Batter should be smooth with no visible lumps.

Pour batter into a Bundt pan. Bake for 40 to 45 minutes or until the top springs back when lightly touched. Remove from oven and allow to cool for 5 minutes. Invert cake onto a serving tray, lightly tapping the bottom of the pan to make sure cake is released before removing pan.

Top with Confectioners Glaze (recipe on page 5).

Orange Cake

1/2 C. vegetable oil
4 C. Master Mix
3 eggs
1/2 C. sour cream
2 tsp. orange zest
1-11 oz. can mandarin oranges,
    coarsely chopped

Preheat oven to 350°. Grease and flour cake pan.

In a large mixing bowl, combine oil, Master Mix, eggs, sour cream and orange zest. Mix on low speed for 1 minute. Stop to scrape the sides of the bowl. Mix again on medium speed for 1 minute. Batter should be smooth with no visible lumps. Stir in mandarin oranges.

Pour batter into a 9"x13" pan. Bake for 30 to 40 minutes or until a toothpick inserted in the center comes out clean.

Peach Upside Down Cake

2/3 C. shortening
3 C. Master Mix
2 egg whites
1 C. buttermilk
1 tsp. vanilla

Topping:
1/4 C. butter, melted
1/2 C. brown sugar
1-15 oz. can peaches, drained

Preheat oven to 350°.

In a large mixing bowl and using two knives, a pastry blender or a wire whisk, cut shortening into the Master Mix until the mixture resembles fine crumbs.

Make a well in the center of the mixture and add egg whites, buttermilk and vanilla. Mix on low speed for 1 minute. Stop to scrape the sides of the bowl. Mix again on medium speed for 2 minutes. Batter should be smooth and no visible lumps.

For the topping, pour melted butter into a 9"x13" pan. Sprinkle brown sugar over the top. Slice peaches in half and fan out over the butter mixture.

Pour batter over the peaches. Bake for 30 to 35 minutes or until a toothpick inserted in the center comes out clean. Remove from oven and allow to cool for 5 minutes. Invert cake onto a serving tray, lightly tapping the bottom of the pan to make sure cake is released before removing pan.

Zucchini Chocolate Cake

1/2 C. butter, softened
3 C. Master Mix
1/2 C. baking cocoa
3 eggs
1/2 C. milk
1 T. vanilla
2 C. grated zucchini
1/2 C. chocolate chips
1 C. chopped walnuts

Preheat oven to 350°. Grease and flour cake pan.

In a large mixing bowl and using two knives, a pastry blender or a wire whisk, cut butter into the Master Mix and cocoa until the mixture resembles fine crumbs.

Make a well in the center of the mixture and add eggs, milk and vanilla. Mix on low speed for 1 minute. Stop to scrape the sides of the bowl. Mix again on medium speed for 1 minute. Batter should be smooth with no visible lumps. Stir in zucchini, chocolate chips and walnuts.

Pour batter into a 9"x13" pan. Bake for 30 to 35 minutes or until a toothpick inserted in the center comes out clean.

Yellow Cake

3/4 C. shortening
4 C. Master Mix
3 eggs
1 C. milk
1 tsp. vanilla

Preheat oven to 350°. Grease and flour cake pan.

In a large mixing bowl and using two knives, a pastry blender or a wire whisk, cut shortening into the Master Mix until the mixture resembles fine crumbs.

Make a well in the center of the mixture and add eggs, milk and vanilla. Mix on low speed for 1 minute. Stop to scrape the sides of the bowl. Mix again on medium speed for 2 minutes. Batter should be light and smooth with no visible lumps.

Pour batter into a 9"x13" pan. Bake for 30 to 35 minutes or until a toothpick inserted in the center comes out clean. You may also pour batter into two 8" round layer cake pans and bake for 25 to 30 minutes or until a toothpick inserted in the center comes out clean.

Rhubarb Cake

1/2 C. margarine, softened
3 3/4 C. Master Mix
1/3 C. brown sugar
2 eggs
1 C. buttermilk
1 tsp. vanilla
1/2 tsp. cinnamon
1 1/2 C. diced rhubarb

Preheat oven to 350°. Grease and flour cake pan.

In a large mixing bowl and using two knives, a pastry blender or a wire whisk, cut margarine into the Master Mix and brown sugar until the mixture resembles fine crumbs.

Make a well in the center of the mixture and add eggs, buttermilk, vanilla and cinnamon. Mix on low speed for 1 minute. Stop to scrape the sides of the bowl. Mix again on medium speed for 2 minutes. Batter should be smooth with no visible lumps. Stir in rhubarb.

Pour batter into a 9"x13" pan. Bake for 35 to 40 minutes or until a toothpick inserted in the center comes out clean.

Carrot Cake

2/3 C. vegetable oil
3 1/2 C. Master Mix
3 eggs
1/4 C. orange juice
1/2 tsp. baking soda
1 tsp. cinnamon
1/2 tsp. cloves
1/2 tsp. nutmeg
1/2 tsp. allspice

1 1/2 C. shredded carrots
1/2 C. crushed pineapple, well drained
3/4 C. chopped walnuts or pecans
3/4 C. raisins

Preheat oven to 350°. Grease and flour cake pan.

In a large mixing bowl, combine oil, Master Mix, eggs, orange juice, baking soda, cinnamon, cloves, nutmeg and allspice. Mix on low speed for 1 minute. Add carrots and pineapple. Mix again on medium speed for 1 minute. Stir in walnuts or pecans and raisins.

Pour batter into a 9"x13" pan. Bake for 30 to 35 minutes or until a toothpick inserted in the center comes out clean. You may also pour batter into two 8" round layer cake pans and bake for 25 to 30 minutes or until a toothpick inserted in the center comes out clean.

Top with Cream Cheese Frosting (page 5).

Red Velvet Cake

3 eggs
1 C. vegetable oil
1 tsp. vanilla
2 to 3 tsp. red food coloring
4 C. Master Mix, divided in half
2 T. baking cocoa
3/4 C. buttermilk

Preheat oven to 350°. Grease and flour cake pan.

In a large mixing bowl, combine eggs, oil, vanilla and red food coloring. Add 2 cups Master Mix and cocoa. Mix on low speed for 1 minute or until combined. Add buttermilk and mix on low speed for 1 minute. Add remaining 2 cups Master Mix and mix on low speed for 1 to 1 1/2 minutes.

Pour batter into a 9"x13" pan. Bake for 30 to 35 minutes or until a toothpick inserted in the center comes out clean. You may also pour batter into two 8" round layer cake pans and bake for 20 to 25 minutes or until a toothpick inserted in the center comes out clean. You may also pour batter into a Bundt pan and bake for 30 to 35 minutes or until the top springs back when lightly touched.

Gold Cake

2/3 C. shortening
3 1/2 C. Master Mix
4 egg yolks
1 C. milk
1 tsp. vanilla

Preheat oven to 350°. Grease and flour cake pan.

In a large mixing bowl and using two knives, a pastry blender or a wire whisk, cut shortening into the Master Mix until the mixture resembles fine crumbs.

Make a well in the center of the mixture and add egg yolks, milk and vanilla. Mix on low speed for 1 minute. Stop to scrape the sides of the bowl. Mix again on medium speed for 2 minutes. Batter should be smooth with no visible lumps.

Pour batter into a 9"x13" pan. Bake for 30 to 35 minutes or until a toothpick inserted in the center comes out clean. You may also pour batter into two 8" round layer cake pans and bake for 25 to 30 minutes or until a toothpick inserted in the center comes out clean.

Apple Spice Cake

1/2 C. vegetable oil
3 1/2 C. Master Mix
2 eggs
1 C. buttermilk
1 tsp. vanilla
1 tsp. cinnamon
1/2 tsp. cloves
1/2 tsp. nutmeg
1 1/2 C. grated or finely
    chopped fresh tart apples
1/2 C. chopped walnuts or
    pecans, (optional)

Preheat oven to 350°. Grease and flour cake pan.

In a large mixing bowl, combine oil, Master Mix, eggs, buttermilk, vanilla, cinnamon, cloves and nutmeg. Mix on low speed for 1 minute. Stop to scrape the sides of the bowl. Mix again on medium speed for 1 minute. Stir in apples and walnuts or pecans.

Pour batter into a 9"x13" pan. Bake for 30 to 40 minutes or until a toothpick inserted in the center comes out clean.

Coconut Crème Cake

2/3 C. vegetable oil
3 1/2 C. Master Mix
1 pkg. (4 serving size) coconut
   crème pudding mix
3 eggs
1 1/3 C. milk
1 C. coconut

Preheat oven to 350°. Grease and flour cake pan.

In a large mixing bowl, combine oil, Master Mix, pudding mix, eggs, milk and coconut. Mix on medium speed for 1 minute. Stop to scrape the sides of the bowl. Mix again on low speed for 1 minute.

Pour batter into a 9"x13" pan. Bake for 30 to 35 minutes or until a toothpick inserted in the center comes out clean.

Top with Chocolate Glaze (recipe on page 4).

Moist Mocha Chocolate Cake

1 C. vegetable oil
4 C. Master Mix
3/4 C. baking cocoa
3/4 C. strong, warm coffee
3/4 C. milk
2 eggs
1 tsp. vanilla

Preheat oven to 350°. Grease and flour cake pan.

In a large mixing bowl, combine oil, Master Mix, cocoa, coffee and milk. Mix on low speed for 2 minutes. Add eggs and vanilla, and mix again on low speed for 2 minutes. Batter should be somewhat thinner than a normal cake batter.

Pour batter into a 9"x13" pan. Bake for 30 to 35 minutes or until a toothpick inserted in the center comes out clean.

Almond Cake

3/4 C. butter, softened
3 3/4 C. Master Mix
2 egg yolks
1 C. milk
1 C. sliced almonds
1 tsp. almond extract
5 egg whites
1/2 tsp. cream of tartar

Preheat oven to 350°. Grease and flour cake pan.

In a large mixing bowl and using two knives, a pastry blender or a wire whisk, cut butter into the Master Mix until the mixture resembles fine crumbs.

Make a well in the center of the mixture and add egg yolks, milk, almonds and almond extract. Mix on medium speed for 1 minute. Stop to scrape the sides of the bowl at least once in the process.

In a separate mixing bowl, beat egg whites and cream of tartar until soft peaks form. With a spatula, take 1/4 of the egg white mixture and fold into batter to loosen. Fold in the remaining egg white mixture.

Pour batter into a Bundt pan or angel food cake pan. Bake for 45 to 55 minutes or until the top springs back when lightly touched. Remove from oven and allow to cool for 5 minutes. Invert cake onto a serving tray, lightly tapping the bottom of the pan to make sure cake is released before removing pan.

Maple Apple Cake

3/4 C. butter, softened
3 1/3 C. Master Mix
2 eggs
3/4 C. pure maple syrup
1 tsp. vanilla
1 1/2 C. grated apples
1/2 C. buttermilk

Preheat oven to 350°. Grease and flour cake pan.

In a large mixing bowl and using two knives, a pastry blender or a wire whisk, cut butter into the Master Mix until the mixture resembles fine crumbs.

Make a well in the center of the mixture and add eggs, maple syrup, vanilla and apples. Mix on low speed for 1 minute or until well combined. Stop to scrape the sides of the bowl. Add buttermilk, and mix again on medium speed for 1 1/2 minutes.

Pour batter into a 9"x13" pan. Bake for 35 to 40 minutes or until a toothpick inserted in the center comes out clean.

Cookies and Cream Cupcakes

2/3 C. vegetable oil
3 1/4 C. Master Mix
3 egg whites, lightly beaten
1 C. milk
1 tsp. vanilla
1 C. crushed Oreos

Preheat oven to 350°.

In a large mixing bowl, combine oil, Master Mix, egg whites, milk and vanilla. Mix on low speed for 1 minute. Stop to scrape the sides of the bowl. Add crushed Oreos, and mix again on medium speed for 1 1/2 minutes.

Spoon batter into greased or paper lined muffin cups. Bake for 18 to 24 minutes or until a toothpick inserted in the center comes out clean.

Molasses Ginger Cupcakes

1/2 C. shortening
3 C. Master Mix
2 eggs
3/4 C. buttermilk
1/2 C. molasses
1 tsp. ginger
1/2 tsp. cinnamon

Preheat oven to 350°.

In a large mixing bowl and using two knives, a pastry blender or a wire whisk, cut shortening into the Master Mix until the mixture resembles fine crumbs.

Make a well in the center of the mixture and add eggs, buttermilk, molasses, ginger and cinnamon. Mix on low speed for 1 minute. Stop to scrape the sides of the bowl. Mix again on medium speed for 2 minutes.

Spoon batter into greased or paper lined muffin cups. Bake for 18 to 24 minutes or until a toothpick inserted in the center comes out clean.

Maraschino Cherry Cupcakes

1/2 C. margarine, softened
3 C. Master Mix
2 eggs
2/3 C. milk
1/3 C. maraschino cherry juice (from jar of cherries)
3/4 C. chopped maraschino cherries
1/2 C. chopped pecans

Preheat oven to 350°.

In a large mixing bowl and using two knives, a pastry blender or a wire whisk, cut margarine into the Master Mix until the mixture resembles fine crumbs.

Make a well in the center of the mixture and add eggs, milk and maraschino cherry juice. Mix on low speed for 1 minute. Stop to scrape the sides of the bowl. Mix again on medium speed for 1 minute. Stir in maraschino cherries and pecans.

Spoon batter into greased or paper lined muffin cups. Bake for 18 to 24 minutes or until a toothpick inserted in the center comes out clean.

Lemon Cream Cupcakes

1 C. butter, softened
3 1/2 C. Master Mix
2 eggs
1 1/4 C. sour cream
2 tsp. lemon zest
1 tsp. vanilla

Preheat oven to 350°.

In a large mixing bowl and using two knives, a pastry blender or a wire whisk, cut butter into the Master Mix until the mixture resembles fine crumbs.

In a separate bowl, combine eggs, sour cream, lemon zest and vanilla.

Make a well in the center of the crumb mixture and add half of egg/sour cream mixture. Mix on high speed for 45 seconds. Stop to scrape the sides of the bowl. Add half of the remaining egg/sour cream mixture, mixing on low speed for 20 to 30 seconds. Add the remaining egg/sour cream mixture, mixing again on low speed for 20 to 30 seconds.

Spoon batter into greased or paper lined muffin cups. Bake for 18 to 24 minutes or until a toothpick inserted in the center comes out clean.

Maple Nut Cupcakes

3/4 C. butter, softened
3 1/2 C. Master Mix
2 eggs
3/4 C. buttermilk
1/2 C. real maple syrup
1 tsp. vanilla
1/2 C. chopped walnuts or pecans

Preheat oven to 350°.

In a large mixing bowl and using two knives, a pastry blender or a wire whisk, cut butter into the Master Mix until the mixture resembles fine crumbs.

In a separate bowl, combine eggs, buttermilk, maple syrup and vanilla and mix thoroughly.

Make a well in the center of the crumb mixture and add half of egg mixture. Mix on high speed for 1 minute. Stop to scrape the sides of the bowl. Add half of the remaining egg mixture, mixing on medium speed for about 20 seconds. Add the remaining egg mixture, mixing again on medium speed for about 20 seconds. Stir in chopped walnuts or pecans.

Spoon batter into greased or paper lined muffin cups. Bake for 18 to 24 minutes or until a toothpick inserted in the center comes out clean.

Pear-Nutmeg Cupcakes

1/2 C. vegetable oil
3 1/4 C. Master Mix
3 egg whites, lightly beaten
3/4 C. milk
1 tsp. vanilla
1 tsp. nutmeg
1 1/2 C. shredded pears

Preheat oven to 350°.

In a large mixing bowl, combine oil, Master Mix, egg whites, milk, vanilla, nutmeg and pears. Mix on low speed for 1 minute. Stop to scrape the sides of the bowl. Mix again on low speed for 1 minute.

Spoon batter into greased or paper lined muffin cups. Bake for 18 to 24 minutes or until a toothpick inserted in the center comes out clean.

Banana Chocolate Kisses

1/2 C. vegetable oil
3 C. Master Mix
2 eggs
3/4 C. milk
1 tsp. nutmeg
1 C. mashed bananas (about 3 bananas)
Approximately 24 Hershey's Kisses

Preheat oven to 350°.

In a large mixing bowl, combine oil, Master Mix, eggs, milk, nutmeg and bananas. Mix on low speed for 1 minute. Stop to scrape the sides of the bowl, then mix on medium speed for 1 minute.

Spoon batter into greased or paper lined muffin cups, filling 2/3 full. Put a Hershey's Kiss inside of each cup, pressing it into the batter until just the tip shows. Bake for 18 to 24 minutes or until tops spring back when lightly touched.

Peanut Butter Cupcakes

1/3 C. vegetable oil
1/3 C. creamy peanut butter
2 eggs
3/4 C. milk
1 tsp. vanilla
3 C. Master Mix
1 C. milk chocolate chips

Preheat oven to 350°.

In a large mixing bowl, combine oil, peanut butter and eggs and beat lightly. Add milk, vanilla and Master Mix. Mix on medium speed for 1 minute or until completely combined. Stir in chocolate chips.

Spoon batter into greased or paper lined muffin cups. Bake for 18 to 24 minutes or until a toothpick inserted in the center comes out clean.

Chocolate Cupcakes

2/3 C. shortening
3 3/4 C. Master Mix
1/3 C. baking cocoa
2 eggs
1 C. milk
1 tsp. vanilla
2 oz. semi-sweet baking
    chocolate, melted

Preheat oven to 350°.

In a large mixing bowl and using two knives, a pastry blender or a wire whisk, cut shortening into the Master Mix and cocoa until the mixture resembles fine crumbs.

Make a well in the center of the mixture and add eggs, milk and vanilla. Mix on low speed for 1 minute. Stop to scrape the sides of the bowl. Mix again on medium speed for 2 minutes. Stir in melted chocolate. Batter should be smooth with no visible lumps.

Spoon batter into greased or paper lined muffin cups. Bake for 20 to 25 minutes or until a toothpick inserted in the center comes out clean.

Allow cupcakes to cool completely. Top with Cream Cheese Frosting (recipe on page 5) and sprinkle with chocolate chips (or shaved chocolate) and toffee pieces, if desired.

Apricot Cupcakes

1/2 C. vegetable oil
3 1/4 C. Master Mix
2 eggs
1 C. apricot nectar
1 C. chopped dried apricots
1 C. white chocolate chips

Preheat oven to 350°.

In a large mixing bowl, combine oil, Master Mix, eggs and apricot nectar. Mix on low speed for 2 minutes, occasionally stopping to scrape the sides of the bowl. Stir in apricots and white chocolate chips.

Spoon batter into greased or paper lined muffin cups. Bake for 18 to 24 minutes or until a toothpick inserted in the center comes out clean.

Pumpkin Spice Cupcakes

2/3 C. vegetable oil
3 1/2 C. Master Mix
2 eggs
1/2 C. milk
1 tsp. cinnamon
1/2 tsp. ginger
1/4 tsp. cloves
1/4 tsp. allspice
1 C. canned pumpkin

Preheat oven to 350°.

In a large mixing bowl, combine oil, Master Mix, eggs, milk, cinnamon, ginger, cloves, allspice and pumpkin. Mix on low speed for 1 minute. Stop to scrape the sides of the bowl. Mix again on low speed for 1 minute.

Spoon batter into greased or paper lined muffin cups. Bake for 18 to 24 minutes or until a toothpick inserted in the center comes out clean.

Allow cupcakes to cool completely. Top with Cream Cheese Frosting (recipe on page 5).

Boston Cream Cupcakes

1/2 C. vegetable oil
3 1/2 C. Master Mix
1 pkg. (4 serving size) vanilla pudding mix
3 eggs
1 1/2 C. milk

Preheat oven to 350°.

In a large mixing bowl, combine oil, Master Mix, pudding mix, eggs and milk. Mix on medium speed for 1 minute. Stop to scrape the sides of the bowl. Mix again on low speed for 1 minute.

Spoon batter into greased or paper lined muffin cups. Bake for 18 to 24 minutes or until a toothpick inserted in the center comes out clean.

Allow cupcakes to cool. Dip tops of cupcakes in Chocolate Glaze (recipe on page 4).

Cranberry Cupcakes

1/2 C. vegetable oil
3 1/4 C. Master Mix
2 eggs
1/2 C. sour cream
1/2 C. cranberry juice
1/2 C. orange juice
1 C. chopped cranberries (fresh or frozen, thawed)
1/2 C. chopped walnuts or pecans

Preheat oven to 350°.

In a large mixing bowl, combine oil, Master Mix, eggs, sour cream, cranberry juice and orange juice. Mix on low speed for 2 minutes, stopping to scrape the sides of the bowl as needed. Stir in cranberries and walnuts or pecans.

Spoon batter into greased or paper lined muffin cups. Bake for 18 to 24 minutes or until a toothpick inserted in the center comes out clean.

Chocolate Chip
Devil's Food Cupcakes

1/2 C. vegetable oil
3 1/2 C. Master Mix
1 pkg. (4 serving size) chocolate devil's
    food pudding mix
2 eggs
3/4 C. water
1/2 C. buttermilk
1 C. chocolate chips

Preheat oven to 350°.

In a large mixing bowl, combine the oil, Master Mix, pudding mix, eggs, water and buttermilk. Mix on medium speed for 1 minute. Stop to scrape the sides of the bowl. Add chocolate chips, and mix again on low speed for 1 minute.

Spoon batter into greased or paper lined muffin cups. Bake for 18 to 24 minutes or until a toothpick inserted in the center comes out clean.

Carrot Raisin Spice Cupcakes

1/2 C. vegetable oil
3 1/2 C. Master Mix
3 eggs
2/3 C. buttermilk
1 tsp. cinnamon
1/2 tsp. ginger
1/2 tsp. cloves
1/2 tsp. allspice
1 C. shredded carrots
2/3 C. raisins

Preheat oven to 350°.

In a large mixing bowl, combine oil, Master Mix, eggs, buttermilk, cinnamon, ginger, cloves, allspice, carrots and raisins. Mix on low speed for 2 minutes, stopping to scrape the sides of the bowl as needed.

Spoon batter into greased or paper lined muffin cups. Bake for 18 to 24 minutes or until a toothpick inserted in the center comes out clean.

Buttermilk Spiced Cupcakes

1/2 C. shortening
3 1/2 C. Master Mix
3 eggs
1 1/3 C. buttermilk
1 tsp. cinnamon
1/2 tsp. nutmeg
1/2 tsp. cloves
1/2 tsp. allspice

Preheat oven to 350°.

In a large mixing bowl and using two knives, a pastry blender or a wire whisk, cut shortening into Master Mix until the mixture resembles fine crumbs.

Make a well in the center of the mixture and add eggs, buttermilk, cinnamon, nutmeg, cloves and allspice. Mix on low speed for 1 minute. Stop to scrape the sides of the bowl. Mix again on medium speed for 2 minutes.

Spoon batter into greased or paper lined muffin cups. Bake for 18 to 24 minutes or until a toothpick inserted in the center comes out clean.

Black Bottom Cupcakes

1/2 C. vegetable oil
3 C. Master Mix
1/3 C. baking cocoa
2 egg whites, lightly beaten
3/4 C. milk
1 tsp. vanilla

Cream Cheese Filling:
1-8 oz. pkg. cream cheese, softened
1 egg
1/3 C. sugar
3/4 C. miniature chocolate chips

Preheat oven to 350°.

In a large mixing bowl, combine oil, Master Mix, cocoa, egg whites, milk and vanilla. Mix on low speed for 2 minutes, stopping to scrape the sides of the bowl as needed.

For cream cheese filling: In a mixing bowl, beat cream cheese until smooth. Add egg and sugar. Mix until well combined. Stir in chocolate chips.

Fill greased or paper lined muffin cups 2/3 full with batter. Place a heaping tablespoon of cream cheese filling inside of each, pressing it down slightly so that cake will bake up around it. Bake for 20 to 26 minutes or until tops spring back when lightly touched.

Berry Lemon Cupcakes

2/3 C. shortening
3 1/2 C. Master Mix
2 eggs
1 C. milk
1 tsp. lemon extract
2 tsp. grated lemon zest
1 C. blueberries (fresh or frozen,
    thawed)

Preheat oven to 350°.

In a large mixing bowl and using two knives, a pastry blender or a wire whisk, cut shortening into the Master Mix until the mixture resembles fine crumbs.

Make a well in the center of the mixture and add eggs, milk, lemon extract and lemon zest. Mix on low speed for 1 minute. Stop to scrape the sides of the bowl. Mix again on medium speed for 2 minutes. Fold in blueberries using just a few quick turns as berries will bleed out juice if over mixed with the batter.

Spoon batter into greased or paper lined muffin cups. Bake for 18 to 24 minutes or until a toothpick inserted in the center comes out clean.

Top with Confectioners Glaze (recipe on page 5).

Pineapple Cream Cheese Cupcakes

1/2 C. shortening
3 1/4 C. Master Mix
3 egg whites, lightly beaten
1/2 C. sour cream
1/2 C. pineapple juice
1-8 oz. can crushed pineapple, drained

Preheat oven to 350°.

In a large mixing bowl and using two knives, a pastry blender or a wire whisk, cut shortening into the Master Mix until the mixture resembles fine crumbs.

Make a well in the center of the mixture and add egg whites, sour cream, pineapple juice and crushed pineapple. Mix on low speed for 1 minute. Stop to scrape the sides of the bowl. Mix again on medium speed for 2 minutes.

Spoon batter into greased or paper lined muffin cups. Bake for 18 to 24 minutes or until a toothpick inserted in the center comes out clean.

Peach Cupcakes

2/3 C. shortening
3 1/2 C. Master Mix
3 egg whites, lightly beaten
1 C. milk
1 tsp. vanilla
1 1/2 C. chopped peaches (fresh or
    canned, drained)
1/2 C. chopped pecans

Preheat oven to 350°.

In a large mixing bowl and using two knives, a pastry blender or a wire whisk, cut shortening into the Master Mix until the mixture resembles fine crumbs.

Make a well in the center of the mixture and add egg whites, milk and vanilla. Mix on low speed for 1 minute. Stop to scrape the sides of the bowl. Mix again on medium speed for 2 minutes. Stir in peaches and pecans.

Spoon batter into greased or paper lined muffin cups. Bake for 18 to 24 minutes or until a toothpick inserted in the center comes out clean.

Sour Cream Fudge Cupcakes

1/2 C. butter, softened
3 C. Master Mix
1 C. sour cream
2 eggs
1/4 C. hot water or coffee
1 tsp. vanilla
3 oz. unsweetened baking chocolate,
   melted

Preheat oven to 350°.

In a large mixing bowl and using two knives, a pastry blender or a wire whisk, cut butter into the Master Mix until the mixture resembles fine crumbs.

Make a well in the center of the mixture and add sour cream. Mix on high speed for 1 1/2 minutes. Stop to scrape the sides of the bowl. Add eggs, hot water or coffee, vanilla and chocolate, and mix again on medium speed for 2 minutes.

Spoon batter into greased or paper lined muffin cups. Bake for 18 to 24 minutes or until a toothpick inserted in the center comes out clean.

Index

How to Use this Book	1
Almond Cake	62
Apple Spice Cake	56
Apple Walnut Upside Down Cake	20
Applesauce Cake	32
Apricot Cupcakes	84
Banana-Coconut Cake	34
Banana Chocolate Kisses	78
Berry Lemon Cupcakes	100
Black Bottom Cupcakes	98
Black Forest Cake	14
Boston Cream Cupcakes	88
Buttermilk Spiced Cupcakes	96
Buttery Chocolate-Chocolate Chip Cake	6
Carrot Cake	50
Carrot Raisin Spice Cupcakes	94
Chiffon Cake	36
Chocolate Bundt Cake	38
Chocolate Cake	30

Chocolate Chip Devil's Food Cupcakes	92
Chocolate Cupcakes	82
Coconut Crème Cake	58
Cookies and Cream Cupcakes	66
Cranberry Cupcakes	90
Frosting & Glazes	4
Chocolate Glaze	4
Confectioners Glaze	5
Cream Cheese Frosting	5
German Chocolate Cake	24
Gold Cake	54
Lemon Bundt Cake	26
Lemon Cream Cupcakes	72
Lemon Pound Cake	12
Maple Apple Cake	64
Maple Nut Cupcakes	74
Maraschino Cherry Cupcakes	70
Master Mix for Cakes & Cupcakes	2
Moist Mocha Chocolate Cake	60
Molasses Ginger Cupcakes	68

Oatmeal Cake	18
Orange Cake	40
Peach Cupcakes	104
Peach Upside Down Cake	42
Pear-Nutmeg Cupcakes	76
Peanut Butter Cupcakes	80
Pineapple Cream Cheese Cupcakes	102
Pineapple Upside Down Cake	8
Pumpkin Chiffon Cake	28
Pumpkin Spice Cupcakes	86
Red Velvet Cake	52
Rhubarb Cake	48
Sour Cream Chocolate Chip Cake	16
Sour Cream Fudge Cupcakes	106
Strawberry Bundt Cake	10
White Cake	2
Yellow Cake	46
Zucchini Chocolate Cake	44

Try all 4 1 Master Mix books!

To purchase more **1**Master Mix books
See Your Local
Gift or Craft Store!

Or call to order a
FREE catalog at
866-804-9892

CQProducts
507 Industrial St.
Waverly, IA 50677

www.cqproducts.com • fax 800-886-7496